We Love Sports Cars

by Katherine Lewis

LERNER PUBLICATIONS ◆ MINNEAPOLIS

Note to Educators

Throughout this book, you'll find critical-thinking questions. These can be used to engage young readers in thinking critically about the topic and in using the text and photos to do so.

Lerner Publications Company
An imprint of Lerner Publishing Group, Inc.
241 First Avenue North
Minneapolis, MN 55401 USA

For reading levels and more information, look up this title at www.lernerbooks.com.

Main body text set in Helvetica Textbook Com Roman.
Typeface provided by Linotype AG.

Editor: Brianna Kaiser
Lerner team: Sue Marquis

Library of Congress Cataloging-in-Publication Data

Names: Lewis, Katherine, 1996– author.
Title: We love sports cars / Katherine Lewis.
Description: Minneapolis : Lerner Publications, 2021. | Series: Bumba books. We love cars and trucks | Includes bibliographical references and index. | Audience: Ages 4–7 | Audience: Grades K–1 | Summary: "Kids who dream of cruising down the highway in a sweet ride need look no further. Readers get a glimpse into the parts of sports cars that make them sleek and special"— Provided by publisher.
Identifiers: LCCN 2020021076 (print) | LCCN 2020021077 (ebook) | ISBN 9781728419268 (library binding) | ISBN 9781728420332 (paperback) | ISBN 9781728419329 (ebook)
Subjects: LCSH: Sports cars—Juvenile literature.
Classification: LCC TL236 .L48 2021 (print) | LCC TL236 (ebook) | DDC 629.222—dc23

LC record available at https://lccn.loc.gov/2020021076
LC ebook record available at https://lccn.loc.gov/2020021077

Manufactured in the United States of America
1-49042-49258-9/8/2020

Table of
Contents

Supercool Sports Cars

Sports cars look good and go very fast. These cars are supercool!

Most people don't use sports cars to get around. Instead, they drive them for fun.

These types of cars have

powerful engines.

A few have electric motors.

Sports cars run on gas,

electricity, or both.

The body of a sports car is low to the ground.

Its curvy design helps air move around the car and makes it go faster!

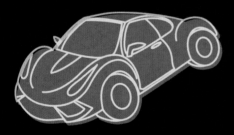

Why do sports cars have a curvy design?

Some sports cars have spoilers.

Spoilers help these fast cars grip the road.

They stay under control.

What does a spoiler do?

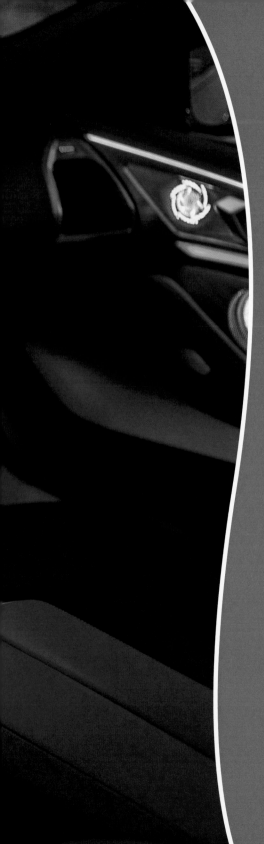

In the past, sports cars were

built only for speed.

Now they have lots of cool tech.

Drivers love their sports cars.

Some race their cars at drag strips.

Where can drivers race their sports cars?

Cars come in flashy colors

such as yellow, red, and blue.

It's supercool to see

a sports car!

Parts of a Sports Car

spoiler

engine

tires

body

Picture Glossary

design

a plan for how a sports car is built

drag strip

a straight track sports cars race on

spoiler

a part of a sports car that helps it stay under control

tech

equipment and tools in a sports car

Learn More

Kenan, Tessa. *Cars.* Minneapolis: Tadpole Books, 2019.

Murray, Julie. *Ferrari F12.* Minneapolis: Abdo Zoom, 2018.

Reinke, Beth Bence. *Race Cars on the Go.* Minneapolis: Lerner Publications, 2018.

Index

Photo Credits